HILLARY AGONISTES

I0141358

Nick Salamone

BROADWAY PLAY PUBLISHING INC
New York
www.broadwayplaypublishing.com
info@broadwayplaypublishing.com

HILLARY AGONISTES
© Copyright 2008 by Nick Salamone

First printing: April 2008
I S B N: 0-88145-380-3

Book design: Marie Donovan
Word processing: Microsoft Word
Typographic controls: Ventura Publisher
Typeface: Palatino

HILLARY AGONISTES was originally presented by Playwrights' Arena (Jon Lawrence Rivera, Artistic Director) and Ginger Perkins and Frantic Redhead Productions at the 2006 Edinburgh International Fringe Festival with the following cast and creative contributors:

HILLARY . . . . Nancy Lindeberg
MORAG . . . . Suze Crowley
CHELSEA/ANTICHRIST . . . . Rebecca Metz
GENERAL/TREASURY/HAWKING/
EVANGELIST/CARDINAL . . . . Nick Salamone

Director . . . . Jon Lawrence Rivera
Stage manager . . . . Ando Iovino
Set design . . . . Ginger Perkins
Sound design . . . . Bob Blackburn
Publicity . . . . Morag Fleming

HILLARY AGONISTES was subsequently presented
by The New York International Fringe Festival,
a production of The Present Company, in association
with Playwrights Arena and Frantic Redhead
Productions with the following cast and creative team:

HILLARY . . . . Priscilla Barnes
MORAG . . . . Jean Gilpin
CHELSEA/ANTICHRIST . . . . .Rebecca Metz
GENERAL/TREASURY/HAWKING/
EVANGELIST/CARDINAL . . . . Nick Salamone

Director . . . . Jon Lawrence Rivera
Assistant director . . . . Clay Storseth
Stage manager . . . . .Jess Manning
Set design . . . . Robert Barbero
Sound design . . . . .Bob Blackburn
Lighting consultant . . . . Jeremy Pivnick
Publicity . . . . David Gersten

The play transferred to the Bleecker Street Theater as
part of the FringeNYC Encore Series, (Britt Lafield,
Producer) with the following cast change:

CHELSEA/ANTICHRIST . . . . Jayme Lake

CHARACTERS & SETTING

HILLARY
MORAG, *to be performed with a Scottish acdent*
GENERAL/TREASURY/HAWKING/EVANGELIST/
  CARDINAL, *to be played by one actor*
ANTICHRIST/CHELSEA, *to be played by one actor*

DISEMBODIED VOICE, *pre-recorded, played over sound
system)*

*The entire action of the play takes place within the
Oval Office of the White House, which should be
expressionistically presented using a large Presidential Seal
projected on the floor down stage of the President's desk.
Furnishings should be simple and in black and white only.
The only other color we see should be the red rim on the pages
of the President's bible and a red phone, both on her desk.*

this play is dedicated to
Dolly Galanti and Anna Conicelli

DISEMBODIED VOICE: June 2. The first day—

(Lights shift, daylight in the Oval Office)

HILLARY: Shoes!!?

MORAG: And clothing.

HILLARY: Clothing?

MORAG: Yes. Skirts, trousers, suits, ties, belts, socks.

HILLARY: Socks?!

MORAG: Under garments.

HILLARY: What?!!

MORAG: In piles.

HILLARY: Piles?

MORAG: Wee Individual piles.

HILLARY: Neat?

MORAG: What?

HILLARY: Tidy?!

MORAG: Tidy?!

HILLARY: Folded?!!!

MORAG: No. Willy Nilly.

HILLARY: Wee willy nilly piles of.clothing?!

MORAG: Bereft of their occupants.

HILLARY: What?????!!!!

MORAG: I'm sorry, Madame President.

HILLARY: How many?!

MORAG: Millions.

HILLARY: Millions!!! Where?

MORAG: Everywhere, Madame President.

HILLARY: *Everywhere?!*

MORAG: Everywhere we've checked.

HILLARY: Baghdad?

MORAG: Yes.

HILLARY: Tehran?

MORAG: Yes.

HILLARY: Mumbai? Beijing?

MORAG: Yes. Yes.

HILLARY: Pyongyang?

MORAG: No word yet.

HILLARY: It must be a *hoax*!

MORAG: A hoax?

HILLARY: Yes, a hoax! Something spread on the internet. Under the radar. So silly we never suspected: At 1:47 P M on Tuesday, June 2, leave a pile of clothing—what you left the house in—down to your skivvies—just leave the pile and—hide yourself, pretend you've disappeared. I don't know—meet somewhere.

MORAG: Naked?

HILLARY: What?

MORAG: Meet somewhere naked?

HILLARY: They'd have brought a change of clothes. For godsake, Morag, work with me here! I'm just saying—isn't it possible that some seemingly innocuous scheme—plans for this scheme—could have been put out there under the radar, something that nobody looking—monitoring—would have caught?

MORAG: How?

HILLARY: A direct mail campaign—the way Bush got in the second term. Four million evangelicals under the radar that nobody counted—was monitoring—believed would come out and pull the lever—poke the chad! —but they did, because somebody got to them—by direct mail or the internet or the pulpit—and nobody knew till it was too late—that it could really happen— not Kerry, not Carville, not *me*. Nobody. Could they have sneaked this...thing...this...this happening...under the radar?

MORAG: This *happening*?

HILLARY: What do the kids call them now—a rave! Word gets out—to the right people—and it happens.

MORAG: But how?

HILLARY: Text messages!! —I don't know! I just said: the internet, the pulpit!

MORAG: In Baghdad? Beijing? Istanbul? Tel Aviv?

HILLARY: You tell me then!

MORAG: I don't know.

HILLARY: Who are they?

MORAG: There are so many.

HILLARY: Is there a *profile*?

MORAG: We don't know yet.

HILLARY: We don't know yet?!

MORAG: It is 1:54 Eastern Standard Time. It's been seven minutes.

HILLARY: Seven minutes!!! That's an eternity. What are we doing? Who are these people, that they would just disappear with out their clothes? Feed the names into the Homeland Security data base and find out what they have in common. Why isn't this being done?

MORAG: Madame President, we don't have all the nam—

HILLARY: The ones we do hav—

MORAG: And some of the Homeland Security personnel—two of the key people—who do this for us—they've vanished too.

HILLARY: What!!!??

MORAG: And...

HILLARY: Yes?

MORAG: And here.

HILLARY: *Here?*

MORAG: *Right* here, Madame President. Janine—

HILLARY: *(Rushing from the room to find Janine)* My own secretary?!!

MORAG: Yes, Madame President.

HILLARY: *(Offstage to a Secret Service agent) (Returning with Janine's girdle)* The entire secret service is out there! I had to wrestle this away from them.

MORAG: The White House is under lock down, Madame President. Vice President Obama has been taken to Safe Haven.

HILLARY: Good.

MORAG: But the Secretary of the Interior is gone.

HILLARY: Oh my God.

MORAG: We believe the Secretaries of Defense, State, Treasury and Labor are still with us.

HILLARY: Thank God.

MORAG: No word from Education and Human Resources, but-

HILLARY: Find out!

MORAG: We are trying, Madame President, but it's slow going. Differentiating the...piles...they all look so very much the same. Ultimately it's about pockets and purses and wallets and the I Ds inside them, isn't it?

HILLARY: Is it!? Ultimately!? Is that what this is about?

MORAG: There are others who appear to be among the...missing...

HILLARY: Oh god oh god, not Chelsea. Dear god, please, not Chelsea.

MORAG: We don't know about Chelsea yet, but Hillary—in New York City...Mister...Mister Clin—

HILLARY: *(Wailing)* Bill!!!!??

(Lights dim quickly. Lights bump up quickly. GENERAL and HILLARY in middle of heated conversation. GENERAL carries a "top secret" file.)

GENERAL: Aliens.

HILLARY: Not terrorists?!

GENERAL: It would be impossible for any terrorist organization to have done this.

HILLARY: But aliens? *That's* possible?! You want me to tell the world that my husband and *millions* of others were abducted by aliens.

GENERAL: You have to tell them something, Madame President.

HILLARY: Clearly, but *this*!

GENERAL: Half of all Americans already believe that aliens monitor us from their U F Os. One in five believes that alien abductions have already taken place. And four million Americans believe that they have already been abducted by aliens *themselves*. Aliens is the way to go on this one, Madame President. The longer you hesitate, the more dangerous the situation grows.

HILLARY: I am not hesitating. I am trying to reason. Is there any *evidence* to support alien abductions.

GENERAL: No.

HILLARY: Don't you think people might *ask* for a little evidence.

GENERAL: We've manufactured some.

HILLARY: And when people—scientists, Congress— bloggers for godsake—examine the evidence— what then?

GENERAL: We'll have at least bought some time to control the situation.

HILLARY: We cannot lie to them.

GENERAL: We're not lying. We have no evidence to the contrary. It's as sound a theory as any. And it has certain advantages.

HILLARY: Advantages?

GENERAL: It will unite people—nations against a common foe.

HILLARY: Extraterrestrial aliens?

GENERAL: And it defuses the...rapture scenario.

HILLARY: Excuse me?

GENERAL: Certain segments of the population are ashamed, Madame President, demoralized. They

feel they have been abandoned by God while their...
more worthy compatriots have been carried off to
heaven by Jesus in the Rapture. Homeland Security
says that in some red states, we cannot get an accurate
account of who is missing. People won't answer their
doors or their phones or show up for work because
they cannot bear the stigma that maybe the Lord didn't
want them.

HILLARY: Oh my god.

GENERAL: Some have even staged their own
disappearances. At 2:48 this afternoon, just minutes
ago—a full hour after everyone else had vanished, the
Reverend Pat Robertson left his car running by the side
of the highway with an Armani suit and a pair of Fruit
of the Loom boxer shorts sitting in a pile on the driver's
seat. We have satellite surveillance of him putting on a
black wig and a mustache, pulling a bicycle out of the
trunk of his Lincoln and pedaling toward Virginia.
The F B I confirms he's in a bunker with the
cryogenically preserved remains of Jerry Falwell
beneath Liberty University in Lynchburg.

HILLARY: Now there's a picture.

GENERAL: We have picked up emails from this bunker
to certain quasi-religious right wing anti-government
para-military groups in Texas and Oklahoma.

HILLARY: What's in them?

GENERAL: Buzz words: Antichrist, Final Conflict,
Armageddon. They seem to be planning something,
though at this point in our surveillance it is unclear
just what. That's why you have to get out in front on
this, Madame President. And channel the country's
fear, its paranoia into something we can control.
If you can sell the country the alien abduction scenario
it will be less susceptible to *whatever* they're plotting.

HILLARY: But—

GENERAL: We must win hearts and minds, Madame President. You cannot wait for people to make up their *own* minds. Be strong. Be clear. Get out in front.

HILLARY: You sound like my husband.

GENERAL: *(Shoots her a look, then:)* I've taken the liberty of preparing some notes. Justifications, interpretations of recent and not so recent events, a rationale that will give credence to the alien abduction scenario.

HILLARY: But General, I don't believe in aliens.

GENERAL: That is beside the point, Madame President.

HILLARY: Is it?

GENERAL: Do you believe in the rapture?

HILLARY: Not all Christians believe in the rapture, General.

GENERAL: Forgive me, Madame President, but that is not an answer.

HILLARY: Why can't we tell them that we simply do not know.

GENERAL: People want certainty, Madame President!! To calm them, to soothe them. Certainty *soothes*! Their friends, their loved ones have been snatched from them. You have to give them something to believe in.

HILLARY: Not if *I* don't believe it!

GENERAL: Do you believe in Armageddon, in Apocalypse? You'd better start, because if you let Robertson and the religious right spin this thing, that's just what you'll get!

HILLARY: How will telling people their loved ones have been abducted by aliens soothe them. They'll want action, they'll want a plan of attack to get them back. They'll be terrified of more abductions.

GENERAL: *(Pulling himself back together, a know-it-all:)* That's all covered in my notes. *(Slapping his "top secret" file down on the President's desk.)* We've poured over the literature. We can contain this.

HILLARY: What literature?

GENERAL: Science fiction of course.

(Lights change)

HILLARY: *(Throwing down the* GENERAL's *"top secret" file notes from the previous scene that she has been reading.)* Klaatu barata nickto!

MORAG: What?

HILLARY: Listen to this: *(Reads prepared speech from the* GENERAL's *notes:)* There is no indication whatsoever that we are under attack by Al Qaeda or any other known or unknown terrorist organization of any stripe. In fact, there is no reason to believe that any— *terrestrial*—power— *(To* MORAG*)* —*terrestrial!!* Are they insane? I can't do it. I won't say it. Aliens!! What do I look like? Patricia Neal?!

MORAG: Who?

HILLARY: Nothing. *(Missing Bill, he would have known who Patricia Neal was)* Oh Bill, where are you?

MORAG: *(Getting the information off her Blackberry)* Chelsea's been located, in Philadelphia, Madame President. She's safe.

HILLARY: Oh, thank God. Thank you, Lord, thank you.

MORAG: One of the secret servicemen assigned to her is gone though—

HILLARY: Triple the detail on her! Quadruple it! And the baby?

MORAG: Safe.

HILLARY: Thank you, Jesus.

MORAG: And her husband.

HILLARY: Good. Thank you, Morag. Make sure she stays put. Oh dear Jesus, watch over her. (*Quick switch of gears, handing* MORAG *the file that the* GENERAL *gave her:*) Shred this. Let's have a go at tonight's address.

MORAG: We've got eighteen minutes before the camera crew is due to arrive.

(MORAG *hands* HILLARY *notes on tonight's address*)

HILLARY: (*From the notes* MORAG *has given her, reads, then out as if to "camera" as lights brighten*) My fellow Americans, as you gather together tonight in your churches or around your dinner tables, in your mosques or in your living rooms, in your synagogues or by your T V sets, rest assured that the strength of our great nation has not been and never will be compromised. Let us place our trust in the institutions of our great and honorable republic to protect and deliver us in this trying time.

(*Lights shift*)

DISEMBODIED VOICE: June 3. The second day—

MORAG: Madam President, we have a problem.

HILLARY: *Another* one?!

MORAG: There's been a leak.

HILLARY: A leak?! About what?!

MORAG: The alien abduction scenario.

HILLARY: That five star son of a bitch! Who'd he talk to?

MORAG: *The New York Times.*

HILLARY: *Who?!*

MORAG: Patrick Healy.

HILLARY: Oh. Tell me everybody thinks it's as stupid as I do.

MORAG: Not quite.

HILLARY: Wha—

MORAG: They're saying the alien abduction scenario originated from the Oval Office. They say it was your idea.

HILLARY: My idea!?

MORAG: That's not all. Mark Souder is about to make a formal resolution to bring forth impeachment proceedings against you to the House Judiciary Committee—

HILLARY: Mark Souder—that creationist from Kansas?

MORAG: Indiana—

HILLARY: Same state. On what grounds?!

MORAG: The illegal breaching of National Security protocols.

HILLARY: But I didn't do anything!

MORAG: Of course you didn't, Madame President.

HILLARY: Wait a minute. This is ridiculous. I'm the President. I decide the National Security Protocols. They're out of their minds!

MORAG: Of course they are, Madam President. The charge can't possibly hold-up.

HILLARY: Of course it can hold up.

MORAG: It's a diversion. It's not an impeachable offense.

HILLARY: Of course it's an impeachable offense. Haven't you learned yet? Anything a goddam majority of the house votes is an impeachable offense is an impeachable offence. Who said that? Somebody said that. Did Bill say that?

MORAG: Gerald Ford, Madame President.

HILLARY: Oh.

MORAG: Madam President, Brownback is speaking on the floor of the Senate. He's calling you a radical Darwinian evolutionist who would rather believe in aliens than in the prophecies of Revelations.

HILLARY: Of course he is! So that's what this is all about. Why didn't the damn aliens do us all a favor and take him. Was this the Republicans' plan all along? Have Army come in here and sell me the alien abduction nonsense and if I buy it they try to impeach me and if I don't buy it they leak it to the press like aliens was my idea and try to impeach me anyway.

MORAG: I don't think so, Madame President. After Iraq, the military no more trusts the Republicans than we do.

HILLARY: Is Carville on this?!!

MORAG: He is, Madame President.

HILLARY: We need a prayer circle.

MORAG: Excuse me, Madam President.

HILLARY: A big one. Have Janine—her replacement—what's her name—the Wellesley woman—

MORAG: Adelaide—

HILLARY: Adelaide, *Adelaide*—have her organize a Woman's Prayer Circle. On the White House lawn—no—the rose garden. Tomorrow morning.

MORAG: But, Madame President, the U N address at nine A M.

HILLARY: We'll pray early

MORAG: Do you think that is wise, Madame President?

HILLARY: Why?

MORAG: What will it accomplish?

HILLARY: What will *anything* accomplish, Morag? It will be a symbol. We will let America—the world—know that we are working to...to handle this-on all fronts.

MORAG: It's risky—

HILLARY: Goddammit, Morag. Don't fight me on this one. Just do it.

MORAG: Yes, Madame President.

HILLARY: Get Downing Street on the phone again. I need to talk to Prime Minister Brown.

MORAG: Right away... *(She punches a number into the red phone on the desk)*

HILLARY: Do we have M-6's updated figures for the U K yet?

MORAG: Roughly six hundred thousand. About a fifth of ours.

HILLARY: Three million Americans. Dear God.

MORAG: Prime Minister Brown will be with you in thirty seconds. *(Looking up M-6's figures in her notes)* The U K numbers line up with the figures we've gotten so far all over. Approximately one percent of the population worldwide—sixty-five million people. Slightly less in Finland, slightly more in Bahrain. *(Into phone:)* Yes, she's right here, I'm handing over. *(To* HILLARY*)* Braveheart for Pocahontas.

*(*MORAG *gives* HILLARY *the phone)*

HILLARY: *(To* MORAG, *responding to the "code names", yanking the phone:)* Goddam Secret Service. *(Into phone:)* Gordon. Have you heard?! They want to impeach me!!

They control Congress again, *of course* they have the votes! Enough to get it to the Judiciary committee and start an inquiry at least. Do they, Morag— Do they have enough for that? Get Carville in here! He probably knows already.

MORAG: Yes, Madame President. *(She exits quickly)*

HILLARY: I should have told the world to go shopping. Isn't that what Bush would have done? "Take that pile of clothing to the dry cleaners, it must be filthy. And when it's all cleaned up, buy it a new suitcase and take it on a trip, that sack of polyester and cotton that used to be your husband." How many in parliament gone? That many? How many Tories? You did better than I did. Any from the house of Lords? None! That figures. Yes, Chelsea's safe in Philadelphia....with her... family, yes. We'll talk tonight about the U N address. Thank you. Alright then. Thank you, Gordon.

(MORAG re-enters. HILLARY hands her the phone.)

HILLARY: What does Carville think?

MORAG: He's still canvassing, Madame President. But right now it's too close to call.

HILLARY: Thank you, Morag. Get him in here as soon as possible. And get Chelsea on the phone, please. Right away.

(Lights shift low and eerie, middle of the night, HILLARY wakes)

HILLARY: Jim? Morag? Jim?

ANTICHRIST: *(Dressed in a black niqab and burqa, wearing a gas mask. The voice is prerecorded and distorted and not the voice of the actress playing Chelsea)*
I am Gog and Magog.
I am the angel of darkness.
I am Yajooj and Majooj

I am Dajjal
I am Destroyer.
I am Rapture and Revelation
I am Apocalypse and Armageddon.

HILLARY: Moorrr—aggggggghh!!! *(She reaches into the desk drawer and grasps an object. She clutches it in her hand throughout the scene)*

MORAG: Are you alright, Madame President?

HILLARY: What do I tell the them, Morag? What do I say? Give them the real figures, of course. Let them hear it from my lips. Sixty-five million persons gone. Bill among them...
the Mumbai telemarketeer slipped out from under her
    headset
the Texan convict stolen from the maw of the electric
    chair
the traitorous Mujahadeen snatched from the firing
    squad wall
the ten year old Senegalese girl swept up before her
    circumcisor's knife
and Janine, poor put-out Janine who never forgave Bill
    for Lewinsky, yet stayed loyal to us both for all
    those years.
Morag, where did they go?

MORAG: I don't know, Hill.

HILLARY: You still think the prayer circle is a bad idea?

MORAG: Oh Hill, you know me. I was brought up a Quaker. We're more reticent about our faith....

HILLARY: You still believe in God, don't you?

MORAG: ...Yes.

HILLARY: Did He do this?

MORAG: I dinna ken, Hillary. I dinna ken.

HILLARY: Well, the Republicans "ken". They "ken" already. Do you believe in aliens?

MORAG: I may believe in 'em. But I don't think they swiped sixty-five million people off the planet without so much as a puff a smoke.

HILLARY: What time is it?

MORAG: Three A M.

HILLARY: Six hours till the U N address.

MORAG: We leave for New York in at seven fifteen.

HILLARY: And the Prayer Circle?

MORAG: Before departure. Dawn. In the Rose Garden.

HILLARY: You added the men I asked for?

MORAG: Edwards. Richardson. Gore.

HILLARY: And Oprah?

MORAG: She'll be there.

HILLARY: Good. We'll get more coverage.

MORAG: The nation will be watching.

HILLARY: Will He be watching—*listening?*

MORAG: Who?

HILLARY: God?

MORAG: I dinna ken.

HILLARY: What's the latest from Carville?

MORAG: *(Her hand on* HILLARY's *shoulder)* Very close. But it doesn't look good.

HILLARY: I can't let them get away with it, Morag. *(Taking* MORAG's *hand,* HILLARY *gives the object she had been holding to* MORAG. *It is a gold cross on a gold chain.)* Help me with the clasp.

(MORAG *places the cross and chain around* HILLARY'*s neck and clasps it*)

HILLARY: The country needs me, I won't be taken down. They won't do to me what they did to Bill. Make sure the camera crews are in place early. Carville had an idea. Before the Prayer Circle I'm going to call their bluff. (*Turning out as if to a camera*) My fellow Americans, the seeming rapture is upon us. (*Slight pause*) Let us pray.

(*Light shift. Daylight, next morning*)

TREASURY: (*Barging past* MORAG) Hillary, what the hell are you doing? You can't say that.

HILLARY: I already have.

DISEMBODIED VOICE: June 4. The third day—

MORAG: (*Unflappably*) Madame President, Secretary of Treasury Bloomsberg wants to speak with you.

TREASURY: (*To* MORAG) —She knows who I am, dear— (*To* HILLARY) People will think it's the end of the world!

HILLARY: Mister Secretary, they already do.

TREASURY: So you confirm their worst fear?! Unfounded and ridiculous as it is, you confirm it?!

HILLARY: I neither confirmed nor denied, Mister Secretary.

TREASURY: But you said it, Madame President. You said the word.

HILLARY: Fuck, Mister Secretary, did I say fuck?

TREASURY: Madame President—

HILLARY: Cunt? Mister Secretary, did I say cunt?

TREASURY: Hillary—

HILLARY: Oh, Mister Secretary, surely you don't think those words have never been spoken before in the Oval Office.

TREASURY: I'm sure I wouldn't know, Madame President. But what has or has not been said *or done* in this office is of no consequence compared to what you have said today to the American public.

HILLARY: All I said—

TREASURY: You said "rapture"—

HILLARY: In a little prayer circle in the middle of the night.

TREASURY: Cut the shit, Hillary. At the crack of dawn before three hundred million Americans, while you were holding hands with Oprah, you said—

HILLARY: Two hundred ninety-seven million, Mister Secretary, two hundred ninety-seven—

TREASURY: You said the word *rapture*. What are they to take that to mean?

HILLARY: The *remaining* two hundred ninety-seven million Ameri—

TREASURY: Oh fucking cunt!

HILLARY: What was that?

TREASURY: I believe I said: oh, fucking, cunt.

HILLARY: Got that off your chest, did you?

(MORAG *exits*)

TREASURY: Forgive me. But, Hillary, if you even hint that the rapture might be some possible explanation for what has happened, you run the risk of destabilizing world markets!

HILLARY: How do you think aliens would have played to the markets? Given the aerospace sector a little goose though, huh?

TREASURY: That's not funny.

HILLARY: I said "seeming rapture", Mike— "seeming". "The seeming rapture has come upon us." That's all I said. Far less than is being screeched on every talk show, italicized in every blog, bold-faced from every headline and gasped at every supermarket check out. For godsake, Mike, let's think this through. You're afraid that your institutional corporate investors will pull their money out of the stock market—

TREASURY: Not just those, the average guy, the individual—

HILLARY: Yes, individuals too—and do what? Cash out and stuff their mattresses?

TREASURY: Panic.

HILLARY: And are they?

TREASURY: We'll know in forty-five minutes, unless you authorize me to close the US markets like the Europeans did.

HILLARY: They shouldn't have. And neither should we.

TREASURY: You've gone out of your fucking mind.

HILLARY: Look at the Asian markets? Beijing! Tokyo! The ones that own us lock, stock and barrel. They've been trading for hours now. They're not collapsing are they?

TREASURY: Not yet.

HILLARY: O ye of such little faith.

TREASURY: In?

HILLARY: In the avarice of man. In the self-interest
of God's children. For heaven sake, Mike, you're a
billionaire—

TREASURY: —Not for long—

HILLARY: —No one is interested in the collapse of
the world economy. The Chinese businessman or the
Japanese banker or the

South Korean manufacturer. They own too much.
Too much of us. Of the American dream. Mister Bush's
ownership society—it's gone global, the Asians heeded
him more than his fellow Americans ever did or could.
Everyone—everyone left that is—has too much at stake.

TREASURY: Just because it hasn't happened in Asia,
doesn't mean it couldn't happen here. The Asians don't
even know what the rapture is, but here! —We've gotta
close the American exchanges—for a few days!

HILLARY: And really set off a panic? I had to get out in
front, Mike.

TREASURY: Out in front of what?

HILLARY: Of the Republicans. I had to at least mention
the word. Put it on the table. Before Robertson and the
rest of the demagogues come out of hiding. I can't have
the world thinking I believe in alien abductions now
can I. They're trying to impeach me, Bloomie.

TREASURY: The assholes are bluffing. They don't even
have the votes for an inquiry.

HILLARY: They do, Mike.

TREASURY: They wouldn't dare. At a time like this.

HILLARY: Carville's never been wrong on a
Congressional head count, Mike. You know how much
they hate me. More than they hated Bill. And they're
afraid. Afraid of this...thing. They want me gone. Even
if it means tearing the country further apart. They have

the votes. Or at least they did before the speech.
Maybe I've bought myself—us—a little time.

TREASURY: Time?

HILLARY: To find an explanation. I haven't given up yet.
Let's keep the markets open for now. Show strength.
It's on my head. To close will do more harm than good.

TREASURY: You're playing with fire, Hillary. And fire
is a dangerous ways to buy time—pandering to the
creationalists! It is not wise to conflate what has
happened with apocalyptic explanations, seeming
or otherwise.

HILLARY: I am not pandering. I am a god-fearing
woman, Mister Secretary. This is a god-fearing nation.

TREASURY: I am a Jew, Madame President. It is not God
I fear. What's next? The Antichrist?—

MORAG: *(Re-entering)* —Madame President, Marine One
is waiting—

HILLARY: —I didn't necessarily mean it literally.

TREASURY: Was this Carville's idea? —For godsake,
Hill, you can't play political word games at a time like
this. A third the goddam country is fundamentalist.

HILLARY: Well they're not very goddam good
fundamentalists are they, Mike, if they're still here?!

TREASURY: What?

HILLARY: *They're still here!*

MORAG: —The U N address—

TREASURY: We heard you!

HILLARY: If it were the literal rapture—not just the
seeming one—then why are they still here? And Bill
and Jane Fonda and fucking Kim Jong-il gone! Kim
Jong-il, Mike! For godsake!!!! What kind of a God

snatches up to his bosom the Stalinist dictator of North
Korea?! What kind of rapture is that?! Of course the
fundamentalists don't really care about North Korea.
They're still obsessed with Bill. That's the beauty part!
That's why the Republicans are acting so crazy! It's not
because they're ashamed that Jesus left them behind.
It's *Bill*!! How do they explain Bill! I swear to God if Bill
hadn't disappeared I would have had the C I A kidnap
him and hole him up somewhere just so I could say
he had. Don't you see, Mike. Bill's our ace in the hole.
No one's going to believe this is the real rapture—least
of all the fundamentalists—if Bill is among the rapt.

(Blackout. Lights change, eeire. HILLARY *has been at her desk
all night, upright, a bible open before her. The bible should
remain open on the Presidential desk for the remainder of the
play.)*

ANTICHRIST: So you bought yourself some time,
have you, woman.

HILLARY: Who are you?

ANTICHRIST: I am that which was and that which will
be, which you heard was coming and now is in the
world. I am Babylon's whore. I am the beast. Woman, it
is the last hour, and as you have heard that I am come,
so now many of us have come. And I among them.

(Lights brighten.)

DISEMBODIED VOICE: June 5. The fourth day—

(MORAG enters and as if awakening HILLARY, says gently:)

MORAG: Madame President, he's here.

HILLARY: What?!

MORAG: The professor.

HILLARY: Yes. Of course. Did you know the bible says
there will be many Antichrists.

MORAG: I know that's what it *says*.

HILLARY: Show him in. Have all my calls held.
And Morag, stay, if you'd like...

MORAG: Thank you, Madame President.

(MORAG *exits and returns with* HAWKING *, immobile in
his wheel chair*)

HILLARY: Hello, Professor Hawking. Thank you.
Thank you for coming to me.

HAWKING: (*Speaking in a flat mechanized voice that seems
to come from a speaker in the back of his wheelchair, the
words seem to be generated by the motion of one hand across
a small keyboard*) You're welcome.

HILLARY: I...I am embarrassed to have inconvenienced
you.

HAWKING: No trouble.

HILLARY: Can I get you anything?

HAWKING: No thank you.

HILLARY: Water?

HAWKING: No.

HILLARY: So.

HAWKING: Yes?

HILLARY: Is there...? Do you have...an...an...explanation?

HAWKING: No.

HILLARY: Oh.

HAWKING: Sorry.

HILLARY: A theory? A hypothesis? A guess?

HAWKING: No.

HILLARY: But is it possible? I mean is there some
possible...scientific...I don't know...some possibility

that...scientifically...something like this...of this magnitude...could have occurred?

HAWKING: Yes.

HILLARY: It is possible?

HAWKING: Yes.

HILLARY: But how?

HAWKING: It happened.

HILLARY: What?

HAWKING: Empirically.

HILLARY: *What?*

HAWKING: It is possible...because it happened.

HILLARY: Oh.

HAWKING: Sorry.

HILLARY: No.

MORAG: What about string theory?

HILLARY: What?

MORAG: String theory?

HILLARY: String theory? Ten dimensions?

HAWKING: Eleven.

HILLARY: Oh.

HAWKING: M.

HILLARY: "M"?

HAWKING: It's M-theory now.

HILLARY: Oh.

MORAG: What does the M stand for?

HILLARY: Yes—

HAWKING: Mother—

HILLARY: Surely not.

HAWKING: Yes. Mother of all theories.

HILLARY: Really?

HAWKING: And mystery.

MORAG: Mystery? Doesn't sound terribly scientific.

HAWKING: No.

HILLARY: Mother and mystery. Oh my.

HAWKING: And membrane.

HILLARY: Membrane?

HAWKING: Yes.

HILLARY: Not a string, but a membrane?

HAWKING: Yes. A straw.

MORAG: A straw?

HAWKING: A string, in ten dimensions. But in eleven, a membrane curved—rolled round on itself. Like a straw.

HILLARY: Oh.

HAWKING: Yes.

HILLARY: Can this M-theory explain—?

HAWKING: No.

HILLARY: No.

(Pause)

HAWKING: I am sorry...about your husband.

HILLARY: Thank you.

HAWKING: Seemingly...dematerialized.

HILLARY: Is that it? Is that what you think? That they've...dematerialized.

HAWKING: Haven't they seemed to?

HILLARY: I don't know. I'm asking you. Matter can't just vanish. Can it. It has to turn into something doesn't it? Ash, carbon, vapor—something. Unless...unless it's simply gone someplace else.

HAWKING: Matter is not an absolute quantity, but an illusion formed by standing waves of energy. The matter that was once William Jefferson Clinton appears to be no more. But the matter of your husband was an illusion all along.

HILLARY: The Republicans would agree with you there.

HAWKING: Of course the same illusory principle applies to them as well. And you. And your Chief of Staff and me. And this office and this world.

HILLARY: So where does that leave us.

HAWKING: Circuitously enough, right here.

HILLARY: But how could this have happened?

HAWKING: I knew until four days ago that the universe was governed by rational laws.

HILLARY: And now?

HAWKING: And now I believe that the universe is still governed by the same rational laws that governed it four days ago. But that my understanding of those laws was more incomplete than I had imagined.

HILLARY: Yes?

HAWKING: Than I could ever have imagined. Until four days ago.

HILLARY: But doesn't what has happened fly in the face of all that you thought—we thought—we knew?

HAWKING: Galileo and Copernicus stole the earth from the center of the universe and flung us into orbit around the sun. But science survived. Thrived. Galileo's correction birthed cosmoo-moo-moo-moo-moo—sorry,

typo—cosmology as we know it. And this event—
physical event—will when we come to understand
it—help us to recalibrate our assumptions about how
matter works—about all we know.

HILLARY: But—

HAWKING: The overwhelming condition of the universe
is order. Until four days ago there was order. Then
an event—or rather sixty-five million separate but
seemingly simultaneous events—then order again.

HILLARY: An act of God?

HAWKING: Physics is the mind of God, Madame
President—

HILLARY: But could this be...a metaphysical
intervention...a direct contradiction of the laws of
science by a...purposeful—a willful —omnipotent...
intelligence?

HAWKING: I don't know.

HILLARY: Could it happen again?

HAWKING: I don't know. I'm sorry, Madame President.

HILLARY: The military suggested aliens.

HAWKING: Surely they knew better.

HILLARY: More strategic than scientific.

HAWKING: Yes.

HILLARY: Illusions, huh?

HAWKING: Yes.

HILLARY: I'm afraid I can't go before the American
people and tell them that.

HAWKING: I wish I had a better answer.

HILLARY: Me too.

(*Lights shift to the eerie blue* ANTICHRIST *light.*)

ANTICHRIST: *(In the black niqab and burqa and gas mask)*
What next Christian? You have been to the centurion
and the money-changer and the star-gazer and still
your hands are empty. Do you turn back to Jesus?
Poor Christ, whom you plug in like a night light to
assuage your fear of the dark. Jesus, lit by a four watt
bulb so little Hillary won't be alone when she wakes
up screaming in the abyss. You live in the void, Hillary
Clinton. It is all illusion. Your god-fearing nation: its
bloated niggers hanging from trees like overripe fruit.
Dragged for miles behind pickup trucks like wedding
cans. A faggot-boy crucified and left to die strapped
to a fence on a purple and majestic mountain.
Rifle-shot-riddled abortionists dead in their driveways.
Your god-fearing geno—and religio—cidal planet
spinning prettily in the emptiness: Janjaweed and
Gypsies. Palestine and Puritans. Cromwell and Croatia.
Dachau and Darfur. I counted every broken skull,
every sluiced bowel, every clutched hand. If that
makes me the Antichrist, I have plenty of company.

HILLARY: Is that who you are?

ANTICHRIST: I am what Chelsea would have been if
she were born in the cradle of civilization and not in
its grave...how's that?

HILLARY: Why are you here?

ANTICHRIST: *(Reaching to embrace* HILLARY*)* I am a
suicide bomber, come to explode us into Paradise,
you too...does that fit?

HILLARY: Are you here to tempt me?

ANTICHRIST: So much temptation in the world, Hillary
Clinton, so much uncertainty. That's why people need
their Jesus, isn't it?

HILLARY: Bill! Bill! Bill! *Morag!!*

(Lights shift, daylight)

DISEMBODIED VOICE: June 6. The fifth day—

MORAG: Come out of hiding have you? We saw the video of you speeding away on your bike in your black wig and moustache. You looked like an illegal alien trying to scoot over the border. Not an image I thought you'd covet.

HILLARY: Morag, the Reverend Robertson is our guest.

EVANGELIST: Must you surround yourself with lesbians, Madame President.

HILLARY: She's not a lesbian, Reverend, she's Scottish.

EVANGELIST: Why is she here?

HILLARY: Because God put her here, of course. You did mean existentially, didn't you?

EVANGELIST: Madame President, your capacity for cleverness does not serve you well in these troubling times.

HILLARY: She is my Chief of Staff, my advisor, and an expert in international affairs in her own right, surely you've done your homework.

EVANGELIST: Why is she in this room?

HILLARY: Because I insist that she be. She is here at my pleasure. As are you.

EVANGELIST: Of course. Forgive me. *(Changing gears)* You were right, Madame President. God would not catch up the living before he has caught up the dead.

HILLARY: I beg your pardon?

EVANGELIST: The apostle Paul is very clear on this. This is a *false* rapture. Else the tombs would have thrown back their doors. The cemeteries ope'd their earthen arms to release the righteous departed first. Therefore I say to you this is a false rapture. The bible makes no mistakes. First God raises up the righteous

dead and then he carries off the righteous *living*. And
since no dead have risen, this is a false rapture.

HILLARY: False.

EVANGELIST: I underestimated you, Madame President.

HILLARY: Did you?

EVANGELIST: You knew all along. You said "seeming
rapture". Seeming: appearing as such but not
necessarily so. You were wary. You were wise.

HILLARY: What was it then, Reverend?

EVANGELIST: Satan, of course.

HILLARY: Satan?

EVANGELIST: Old Nick has taken his conscripts.

HILLARY: Drafted? Sixty-five million? That's quite
a battalion.

EVANGELIST: Yes. Kim Jong-il. Hanoi Jane.

HILLARY: My husband.

EVANGELIST: Exactly.

HILLARY: But why?

EVANGELIST: To be footsoldiers, of course.

HILLARY: Of course.

EVANGELIST: In the army of darkness.

MORAG: Oh, horsepiss.

EVANGELIST: Must I be disrespected by a godless
Scotswoman, Madame President?

HILLARY: Forgive her Reverend. She's a Quaker.
Foot soldiers, you say? I can't see Bill as a foot soldier.
Surely he's made lieutenant by now.

EVANGELIST: You are either with us or against us, Madame president. You have shown yourself to be a woman of wisdom. You must make a choice.

HILLARY: A choice?

EVANGELIST: Between good and evil. Between our army and theirs.

MORAG: You have an army too? You and your paramilitarist friends.

HILLARY: Morag.

EVANGELIST: Not my army. God's army. Will you join us against the sixty-five million minions of Magog. Against the forces of darkness. Against the prince of the power of the air. Satan has chosen his conscripts! It is time to choose the Lord's!

MORAG: But these people—sixty-five million—they're gone. There's no evidence, no...justification, no... possible rational...

EVANGELIST: (To MORAG) You Europeans! You still insist in living in a world of reason. Reason with the Saddams. Reason with the Ayatollahs. Reason with the Ahmadinejads. And you reason with the devil! The age of reason is over! Your enlightenment has long since dimmed. You and your reality-based Rasputins standing in the quicksand of Descartes and Rousseau. Clutching your humanist mantel about you like a fig leaf, like the emperor's new clothes. You should get down on your knees and thank Jesus that He has brought you to a country beyond reason. (To HILLARY) End times is here, Mrs Clinton. I am offering you a lifeline. A place in the hierarchy. You could sway millions and bring them to the glory of the Lord.

MORAG: But they're gone! Gone! The sixty-five million. There are no foot soldiers. No army. Just sixty-five million piles of cloth and leather.

EVANGELIST: That they are naked and invisible does not make them any less potent. Indeed, it is their nakedness and their very transparency that makes them such a danger. The devil is wily, woman. He knows the ways of the world.

MORAG: So this is it... What you and that frozen corpse have cooked up to save face—

HILLARY: —Morag—

MORAG: —To weasel your way back in. Back to power. Back to influence. Demonize the vanished, blacken their very souls. Sow the seeds of hysteria and panic and march us all to Armageddon.

HILLARY: You must forgive her, Reverend.

EVANGELIST: That's quite alright. After all...you have been abandoned, Madame President...by your apostate daughter and your godless sp—

MORAG: You leave Chelsea out of this—

EVANGELIST: —Abandoned by your infidel child and your adulterous spouse. Only God opens his arms to you. Will you walk towards your Creator and embrace Him? You could lead this nation back to righteousness. The clash of civilizations is enjoined. You are at a crossroads, Hillary Clinton. The paths fork here. Acknowledge what every true American knows in his heart of hearts, can see with his own eyes: the Antichrists are amongst us, woman, their number is legion: the suicide bomber, the fratricidal cleric— they are the children of the beast. You can be the handmaiden of the lord—or you can be the whore of Babylon! It is time to decide on whose side you shall march in the great battle, for make no mistake Armageddon is upon us.

(Light shift. HILLARY *alone in a pool of light)*

HILLARY: *(In extremis, searching)* The Antichrist appears to me...but it seems as sane as you, Bill. Or me. The nation, Bill...we're spinning in the void. Sleepless in the long black night. It's not just me. C N N says fifty-eight percent of the population has hardly slept in five days. Out of despair. The age of reason...*is* over. I have to give them something, Bill, something to believe in, a night light against the dark...

(Bright T V lights)

HILLARY: My fellow Americans, we must be strong, we must be vigilant. The antichrists are among us, their number is legion...

(Light shift, red demonic)

ANTICHRIST: *(Bellowing, reverberative, in black niqab, burqa but no gas mask)* I bring fire, woman. I bring roaring and the gnashing of teeth. I am lion, I am serpent, I am goat. I am the daughter of Jerusalem, handmaid of Allah, Chimera and Sphinx and kamikaze patriot. Suicide bombadeer. Ash'hadu an la ilaha il-Allahu, wa-ash'hadu anna Muhammadan 'abduhu wa rasooluh. And I am come.

(ANTICHRIST pulls the niqab and gas mask from her face.)

(Light shifts to daylight Oval Office preset)

CHELSEA: Antichrist?!!!

HILLARY: What are you doing here?!

DISEMBODIED VOICE: June 7. The sixth day.

CHELSEA: I am your daughter.

HILLARY: Don't you know it isn't safe?

CHELSEA: Safe. Here in the White House?

HILLARY: For you to travel. You should have stayed in hiding. There have been death threats. Thousands of

death threats. Against you. And your husband.
You could have been killed!

CHELSEA: I wasn't. Not everyone has been so lucky.
Thanks to you...

HILLARY: Did you think you'd be somehow less
conspicuous in your Burqa?

CHELSEA: That doesn't deserve an answer.

HILLARY: Did he come with you?

CHELSEA: No. He's with the baby. Where you sent us.
I wouldn't go. I had to come here.

HILLARY: It never should have been permitted.

CHELSEA: I'm a citizen like all my fellow Americans.
I have rights that neither you nor your agents can
abrogate.

HILLARY: You talk like you are a political prisoner.

CHELSEA: Do I? Well—

HILLARY: I am trying to protect you and my
granddaughter.

CHELSEA: And your son-in-law?

HILLARY: Yes, of course. At least he had the sense to
stay put.

CHELSEA: How could you? "The antichrists are among
us, their number is legion."!!! How could you say that!?
What are you doing?

HILLARY: I am trying to lead the nation in it's hour of
gravest uncertainty.

CHELSEA: Leadership? It's demagoguery. The
antichrists? You don't believe that.

HILLARY: I used the word exactly once. As a metaphor.

CHELSEA: A metaphor for what? Muslims?

HILLARY: For extremist, for godsake. For militants—
terrorists—*of every stripe.*

CHELSEA: For Christian militants as well?

HILLARY: Precisely. Just vague enough. I didn't mean—

CHELSEA: Christian fundamentalists? Do you think any
Christians felt chastened when you bellowed
"antichrists"?

HILLARY: I did not bellow. It was one word, one quiet
word in a reasoned speech of a thousand words.

CHELSEA: Well that's not how it played on any of the
networks. That's not how it played on *Fox.* What do
you think people *heard*??? Don't you know how some
of your fundamentalist citizenry define Antichrist??
Anybody that doesn't believe the way they do. Well
that's me, Mother, me and every Muslim and every
Jew and every Buddhist and every Hindu on the planet.
What in the name of heaven were you thinking.

HILLARY: I am doing the best that I know how.

CHELSEA: You are inflaming right wing religious
zealots!!!

HILLARY: Could I inflame them anymore than my
only daughter, the daughter of the president of the
United States—two presidents of the United States—
converting to Islam four months after her mother takes
the oath of office? Look at you. You think Robertson
and Dobson don't call you or your *husband* religious
zealots.

CHELSEA: And what do you call us?

HILLARY: I am trying to hold the country together.
To mete out a balm. To do my duty.

CHELSEA: Whatever happened to conscience and
conviction and respect for the beliefs of others you
ran so hard on.

HILLARY: I had to run on something after you hijacked my entire election campaign with your engagement to a Sunni from Dubai.

CHELSEA: I thought you were proud of me.

HILLARY: That was your father. I didn't have time to be proud. He didn't have to run for President in a nation torn asunder by a misbegotten war and religious intolerance and fear. And he doesn't have to find a way to stitch it back together in the face of the inexplicable.

CHELSEA: Ash'hadu an la ilaha il-Allahu. Something has happened that is *inexplicable*! So why must you rush to explain what only Allah knows. There are some things not meant for man to comprehend. Would you bring on calamity in your misguided rush for certainty.

HILLARY: No one wants to hear that we do not have answers. No one wants to hear that we are not in control.

CHELSEA: Control is an illusion. An illusion of the West. Of modernity.

HILLARY: That's what you'd like me to go before the American people and say?!

CHELSEA: It would be better—it would be truer— than what you have already said. Antichrists!?

HILLARY: I have to talk in a way that people will understand.

CHELSEA: So you talk like Bush? Is that the only way you think that people understand?

HILLARY: I have to be clear. And strong.

CHELSEA: And preach Armageddon!? You are letting them turn this...this...

HILLARY: Yes—go ahead—tell me, my dear *God*, Chelsea, *please* tell me—this *what*?

CHELSEA: This...inexplicable thing...that has happened...into a religious war. Right here. Twenty-six mosques have been attacked. Imams slaughtered in their homes like Sharon Tate. Women wearing burqas raped and mutilated and left to die in alleyways and parking lots. Just last night since you cried Antichrist, Fajir, the midwife at the birth of your granddaughter was gutted like a deer—

HILLARY: —Oh no—

CHELSEA: —Her killers smeared 6-6-6 on her doorstep with her own bowels. Are you getting the details in your little briefings. Is anything real getting through??! Yes I'll wear this Burqa till it falls in threads off my body. I'll never take it off not even to bathe until this stops. You make this stop. This is not how you taught me the world is supposed to be. Not here. Not in my country. You make this stop. Do something. Say something, Mother. Make it stop.

HILLARY: This is a Christian nation.

CHELSEA: This is not a Christian nation, Mother. It is nation founded by Pilgrims fleeing religious persecution and yearning to live in a land where they were free to worship however they chose. A nation whose constitution demands the separation of church and state. I am a part of this nation, Mother. And I am not...I am no longer...a Christian.

HILLARY: Please, Chelsea, please don't say—

CHELSEA: And now at the worst possible time in the worst possible way you are imposing on us all some deadly Apocalyptic Dogma.

HILLARY: Chelsea, you don't understand. I am trying to protect you. Protect us all.

CHELSEA: Protect us all from what?

HILLARY: From the abyss.

CHELSEA: What?!

HILLARY: Chelsea. There are sixty-five million people vanished.

CHELSEA: There are six billion five hundred million people who haven't.

HILLARY: And all of them on the verge of hysteria, just waiting...waiting...waiting....

CHELSEA: For what? It's already happening, Mother. I'm not going back into hiding. I'm going to speak out.

HILLARY: No. No Chelsea. It is too dangerous.

CHELSEA: I'm not afraid of danger.

HILLARY: Where? Where are you going? At least let me—

CHELSEA: It's in God's hands now. I trust him to work through me. If only you trusted as much for yourself.

HILLARY: Where are you going??! It's not safe!!!! You could be killed.

CHELSEA: Bismi Allahi alrrahmani alrraheemi.
The Quran, chapter 31, verse 34: Verily the knowledge of the hour of judgment is with God alone. It is He Who sends down rain, and He Who knows what is in the wombs. Nor does anyone know what it is that he will reap on the morrow. Nor does anyone know in what land he is to die.

HILLARY: Goddam it, you tell me where you are going or I'll have you locked up!

CHELSEA: Back to Philadelphia. There's a peace vigil in Independence Plaza beneath the Liberty Bell. We won't be scapegoated, Mother. I'm only the Antichrist if you say I am.

(Light shift

MORAG: Madame President. Defense is in the war room. Intelligience has confirmation. Iran has a nuclear warhead with the launching capability to strike Tel Aviv within minutes. Tehran has delivered an ultimatum. The Ayatollah Khamenei has issued a fatwa calling for your assassination. He calls you Dajjal—the Dark Messiah—The Antichrist.

HILLARY: And so it begins.

MORAG: What?

HILLARY: Armageddon.

(Light shift.)

CARDINAL: Armageddon?

DISEMBODIED VOICE: June 8. The seventh day—

HILLARY: The Iranians have threatened Israel with their spanking new nuclear bomb, Your Eminence. Surely Ahmadinijad's bellicosity did not go unnoticed at the Vatican.

CARDINAL: Surely not, Madame President.

HILLARY: When a rogue nation threatens a sovereign state with nuclear annihilation, isn't that Armageddon?

CARDINAL: Hiroshima, Nagasaki. Such lovely names. Your nation has more than *threatened* a sovereign state with nuclear annihilation, Madame President. Yet no responsible person then said Armageddon had begun.

HILLARY: I will not be the whore of Babylon

MORAG: Excuse me. I can be of no use to you here. *(She exits, pointedly)*

CARDINAL: Your Chief of Staff seems disheartened.

HILLARY: I can't help that.

CARDINAL: In some fundamentalist circles Rome is the new Babylon and his Holiness, Babylon's new whore.

HILLARY: So I've been told.

CARDINAL: Your friend, Mister Robertson and his ilk—they are happy to bedfellow with us for political gain: against abortionists, against sodomites, but that is where they draw the line. They fear the church's power, it's history, it's function as preserver of culture and art. Our pantheistic Greeks, and poly-theistic Romans. The fundamentalists say we are purveyor of paganism! After all, our beloved Erasmus was the first humanist. And you know how much it is they cannot abide humanism, secular or otherwise. And of course the Renaissance. They would just as soon live in a world without the Renaissance—if you could call life on earth without the Renaissance living.

HILLARY: Mustn't forget Torquemada.

CARDINAL: Every religion has its Torquemadas, Madame President. The trick is to avoid becoming a faith where every co-religionist *is* a Torquemada.

HILLARY: I'll keep that in mind.

CARDINAL: Tomorrow the Holy Father will address the world from his window and proclaim the disappearance of the multitudes a miracle—*miracolo.*

HILLARY: A miracle? Don't miracles happen for a purpose? The lame walk, the blind see, the lepers are rendered whole.

CARDINAL: Who can know the mind of God, Madame President?

HILLARY: There are those who say what you would call a miracle is the devil's work. Surely you've heard. They say the devil has conscripted his army: sixty-five

million strong, my secretary...my husband...among
them.

CARDINAL: And two cardinals, nine archbishops,
twenty-one bishops, eleven abbots, five abbesses,
fifty-seven friars, one hundred and twenty-one monks,
one hundred and sixty-four nuns. And two hundred
and forty-five priests. May they rest in peace.

HILLARY: A miracle is not an answer to that. If there is
a war, your Eminence, between the power of light and
the power of darkness, we must know which is which
and where we stand. We are not talking about water
turned to wine or multiplying loaves and fishes.
Sixty-five million people are gone. Maybe in Rome
or Paris or London talk of miracles makes that
comprehensible but not here, your Eminence, not here.

CARDINAL: When the earth shook and opened itself and
swallowed whole peoples—when the sun disappeared
in the noonday sky—our earlier selves had no way to
comprehend that which we take for granted now.

HILLARY: *One percent* of the entire—

CARDINAL: The Bubonic plague stole half of Europe—
half! And did the Popes or Dante or Petrarch march us
into the abyss? No! They pulled us from the brink. Not
with incendiary conjecture, but with literature and art—

HILLARY: But doesn't the bible say—

CARDINAL: The bible says many things, Madame
President, all capable of great and dangerous
misinterpretation.

HILLARY: *(This has been haunting her the entire play,
she lets him have it:)* What kind of God would eliminate
sixty-five million people in the blink of an eye. That's
not God, that's a diabolical terrorist on a cosmic scale.

CARDINAL: *(To comfort her)* Oh my child, it's better than
the kind of God we've always had. More direct and
much improved. World War II took fifty million. Mao
in China alone and mostly through famine, another
forty million. AIDS, twenty-seven million and counting.
The Influenza Pandemic of nineteen eighteen and
nineteen wiped out three percent of the human beings
on this planet. Last century's grimmest harvests. And
so much suffering. Now, in this new century, sixty five
million taken—one percent—and so mercifully, so
painlessly. And so forthrightly—no intermediaries
working on God's behalf to muddy the waters. No one
can blame Hitler or Mao or homosexuals or microbes
for this one. And so swiftly, no one living in terror of
its coming. I say God is learning. After—what—how
many millennia! Finally He shows His genius! Let's
hope something better comes of it than Armageddon!

HILLARY: Who are you?

CARDINAL: I am a wily old sexless faggot, Mrs Clinton.
Finocchio. I have survived the wilds of the witchhunts
and the wickets of didacticism under the billowing blue
Tintoretto canopy of Mother Church. I have survived
history. And I—and the Holy Father—we are offering
you a way to survive it too.

HILLARY: You and the Holy Father do not have to
contend with the religious upheaval that rocks my
country.

CARDINAL: The world has often had to contend with the
upheavals-religious and otherwise—that have rocked
your country.

HILLARY: There is no certainty in *miracles*, your
eminence! I cannot offer my country talk of miracles
in the face of nuclear holocaust!

CARDINAL: There is no certainty in the *world*, Hillary
Clinton! Clearly *il miracolo di Dio* has taught us that

much. Certainty is an illusion. A cosmic folly that has
lost its potency. What a relief! We are closer to truth,
because now we know how very far away from truth
we have been. It is time, Madame President. Time for
rebirth. A new Renaissance. *Rinasciemento.* In the wake
of the Black Death—with half of Europe gone—a new
world was born. What will this new act of God bring
into the world? You get to decide this time. You have
been presented with a choice, my child. And it was not
the choice you thought. Not light and dark or good
and evil. But life and death. You can chose miracles—
miracoli—or you can chose Armageddon. Truth or
illusion, Hillary Clinton, life or death.

(CARDINAL *exits. Light shift.*)

DISEMBODIED VOICE: June 9. The eighth day—

CHELSEA: Thank you for joining us here, my friends,
on this bright Spring morning, beneath the Liberty Bell,
in this city where our founding fathers held their first
congress and crafted the Declaration of Independence.
My own father, may he be with Allah, I know, would
be proud of us today for standing together here as we
do now, a sea of faces: brown and black and yellow and
red and white, Christian, Muslim, Buddhist, Jewish,
Hindu. A sea of peace. Some have belittled our efforts
today, calling our solemn vigil an "Anti-Armageddon"
rally—as if that were a bad thing, my friends. For
these benighted individuals and for those in the
Congress and the White House and the Great Halls
and Parliaments of this world, for leaders everywhere
of every possible sympathy, persuasion and
disposition, that they should be visited with wisdom
in these dangerous hours, let us pray:
Bismi Allahi alrrahmani alrraheemi
Praise be to God, The Cherisher and Sustainer of the
    world
Most Beneficent, Most Merciful, Master of the Day of

Judgement
Thee alone do we worship and Thine aid we seek
Show these men—these women—show us all—the
   straight path
The path of those on whom Thou hast bestowed Thy
   grace
The path of those whose portion is not wrath
The path of those who do not go astray
In the name of Allah, most gracious, most merciful,
Bismi Allahi alrrahmani alrrahhhhhhhhh—

*(The deafening sound of an explosion intermixed with
bloodcurdling screams. Blackout. A horrible stillness)*

(Lights up)

MORAG: Madam—Hillary...Hill...Chelsea... She's dead,
Hill, she's dead.

HILLARY: Vanished? You mean disappeared!?

MORAG: No, Hill, she's dead. There's been a bomb...
a suicide bombing at Independence Plaza... Forty-nine
dead so far...nuns, priests, a Bishop... Rabbis, Imams,
six Buddhist monks...there's panic all over. C N N
was carrying the vigil live... There's footage...

HILLARY: Oh God, oh God. Oh God. But her
bodyguards, the secret service, where were th—?

MORAG: They're all dead too. Chelsea was near
the...origin of the explosion.... They think it must
have been someone she knew. They've located...her...
remains. She's being airlifted. The helicopter will come
here directly.

HILLARY: My granddaughter?

MORAG: No word yet.

HILLARY: Her husband?

MORAG: We just don't know yet.

HILLARY: Dear God.

(There is the sound of church bells, then over the bells, the sound of prayers of mourning in Arabic, then in Latin, then in Hindi. Through all this there is the sound of distant explosions growing closer and a faint rumble that as it becomes louder is the sound of rioting and chaos. HILLARY sits motionless.)

MORAG: Madame President? Army—

HILLARY: Send him in.

(MORAG exits.)

GENERAL: *(Entering)* I'm sorry, Madame President—

HILLARY: Thank you.

GENERAL: Ahmadinijad's done it, Madame president.

HILLARY: Chelsea? He's killed Chelsea? Is he the one?

GENERAL: No, Madame President. Iran has launched its Shihab-4 nuclear warhead at Tel Aviv. Israel has deployed its anti-ballistic missile defense system to intercept and destroy the incoming Shihab.

HILLARY: Dear God.

GENERAL: The Israeli's have counter—attacked, Madame President. Their Jericho-3 thermonuclear payload will strike downtown Tehran in nine minutes. The Iranians have no realistic defense against it.

MORAG: *(Entering quickly)* Anti-Islamic rioting is breaking out in Dearborn and Detroit. At least eight hundred are dead and thousands injured.

HILLARY: Mobilize every American and NATO missile defense system in the region. Blow the goddam Shihab *and* the Jericho out of the sky.

GENERAL: Yes, Madame President. *(He exits)*

MORAG: You have to speak out, Madame President. You have to—now.

HILLARY: I—I can't—

MORAG: There is no time, Madame President.

HILLARY: I—

MORAG: Hillary: Now. It must be now! *(From her Blackberry)* The riots are spreading to Richmond and Dallas and Falls Church and Salt Lake City—Hillary, now...cameras...rolling...you can do this...in three—

HILLARY: Just give me—

MORAG: Two—

HILLARY: Gold help me—

(MORAG gestures "one")

HILLARY: My fellow Americans...I...come before you...

(The GENERAL enters carrying a body bag in which are the unweildy remains of CHELSEA's body. Perhaps her bloodied veil is available to HILLARY beneath the zipper. The GENERAL places the body bag across he Presidential desk atop the open bible as if it were a bier and exits.)

HILLARY: ...Oh dear God, my baby—my butterscotch— my little girl— *(She picks up the body bag and cradles it to her breast, rocking and keening)* What have I done—

MORAG: Hillary...

HILLARY: Oh dear God... My...my fellow...my fell... *(Silence)* Nor does anyone know what it is that he will reap on the morrow. Nor does anyone know in what land he is to die. *(Silence)* Oh dear

God, forgive me... *(Long pause. Regaining composure but something has shifted in side her:)* Revelation, chapter 22: And he showed me a pure river of water, clear as crystal...and in its midst was there the tree of life, which

bare all manner of fruit... *(Holding* CHELSEA *to her)*
...and the fruit of the tree was for the healing of
nations... *(Slight pause, terrible admission:)* —I have *no
idea* how much time remains for us—before we are
taken or left—before the Antichrists come or they
don't—before the final rapture or rupture in this our
life. But until such time—let us wash in that pure river,
clear as crystal, let us join hands to surround and
protect that tree, that tree of life, of all our lives, our
little history of human lives on this good earth. Let us
step back from cataclysm, from...Apocalypse, from the
abyss. Let us not be foot soldiers in an... *(Barely able to
say the word)* ...Armageddon of our own making. Let us
stand together in the face of...*uncertainty*...and lay down
our swords, our words, our *illusions*—our atomic fire
and our nucleic ice and agree to just that much.

*(The lights darken slightly, the Presidential Seal that is
projected on the floor glows. A brilliant white light pulses
throughout the theater for three beats. The lights dim slowly
to black.)*

END OF PLAY